WAYNE
GRETZKY

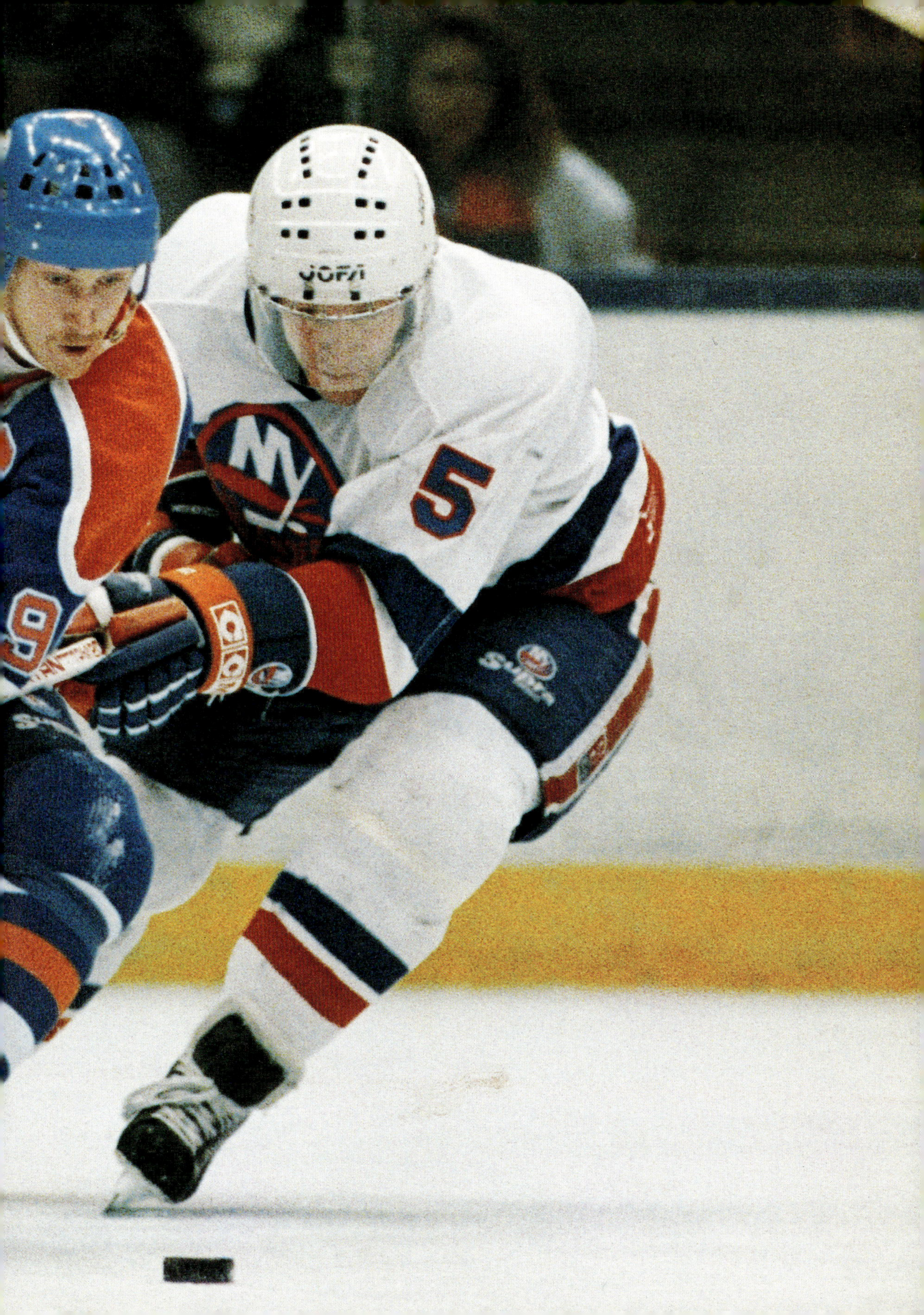
JOFA
5

(Photo on front cover.)
Wayne Gretzky takes dead aim in a game against the Chicago Blackhawks.

(Photo on previous pages.)
Wayne Gretzky and the New York Islanders' Denis Potvin (5) jostle for a loose puck.

Text copyright © 1996 by The Child's World, Inc.
All rights reserved. No part of this book may be reproduced or utilized in any form or by any means without written permission from the Publisher.
Printed in the United States of America.

Photography supplied by Wide World Photos Inc.

Library of Congress Cataloging-in-Publication Data
Rambeck, Richard.
Wayne Gretzky / Richard Rambeck.
p. cm.
Summary: Narrates a series of wins by the hockey champion who was named NHL's Most Valuable Player every year from 1980 to 1987 and who was dubbed "The Great One."
ISBN 1-56766-203-X (lib. bdg.)
1. Gretzky, Wayne, 1961- —Juvenile literature.
2. Hockey players—Canada—Biography—Juvenile literature.
[1. Gretzky, Wayne, 1961- . 2. Hockey players.]
I. Title
GV848.5.G73R36 1995   95-5624
796.962'092 B—20   CIP
                                AC

WAYNE GRETZKY

BY RICHARD RAMBECK

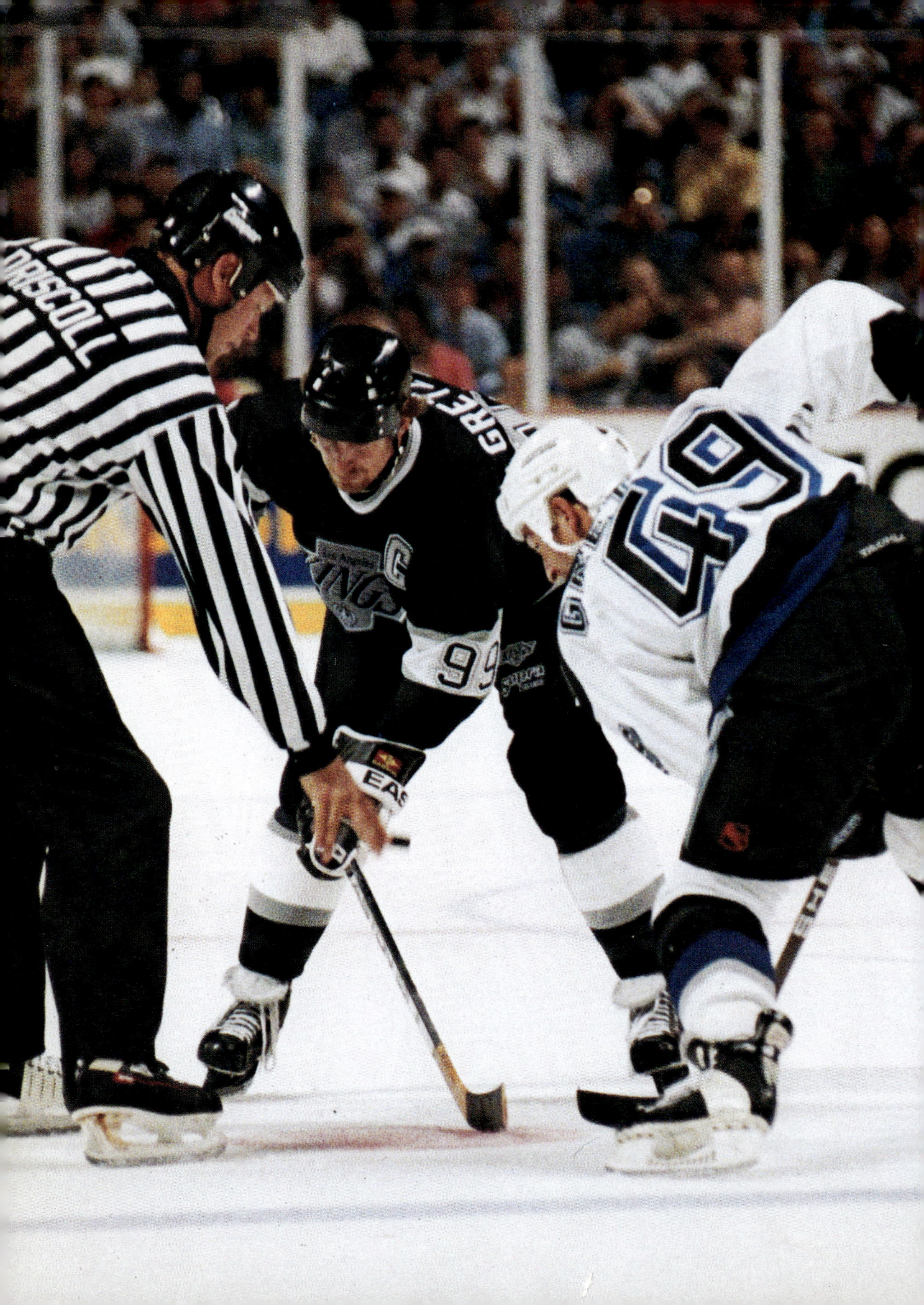
99

The Los Angeles Kings Wayne Gretzky faces off against his brother Brent (49).

Wayne Gretzky had a big smile on his face. He had just finished leading his team, the Los Angeles Kings, into the 1992–93 National Hockey League championship series. To get to the finals, the Kings defeated the Toronto Maple Leafs in an amazing seven-game series. Trailing three games to two, the Kings got a game-winning goal in overtime from Gretzky to tie the series. Then he scored three goals in the seventh game.

"That was one of the best games I've ever seen him play," Kings forward Luc Robitaille said of Gretzky. The Los Angeles star had personally carried the

Kings to victory. In addition to his three goals in the seventh game, Gretzky also had an assist in the 5–4 victory. "I don't think I've ever had as much personal satisfaction," Gretzky said. He was happy because he had done what most people thought he couldn't do anymore.

Gretzky missed half of the 1992–93 season because of a back injury. When he returned to action, he scored only 16 goals in 45 games for Los Angeles. The experts said that Gretzky, who was only 31 years old, was no longer a great player—that he was no longer worthy of his nickname, "The Great One." Once the

Gretzky pursues a loose puck.

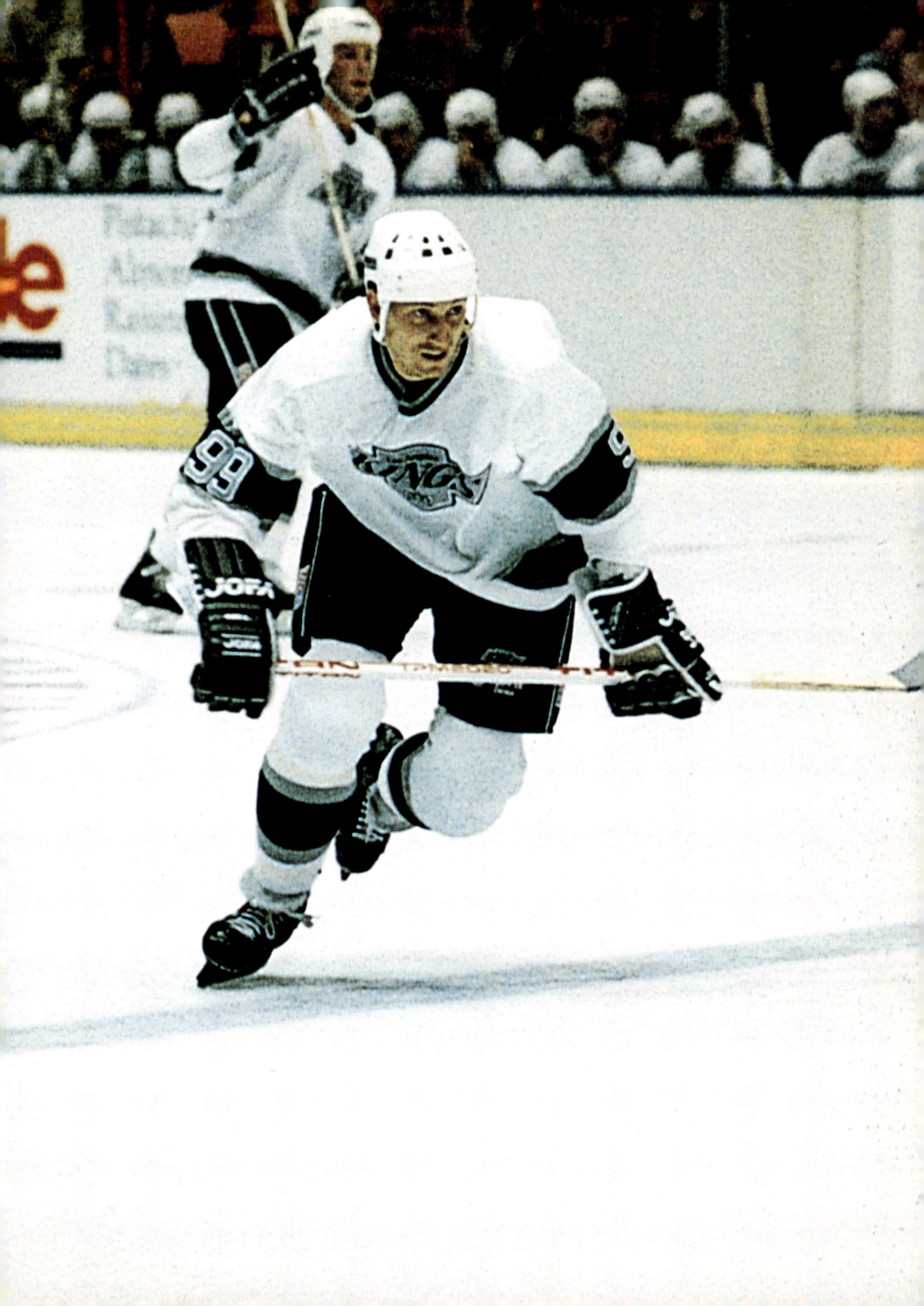
99
JOFA

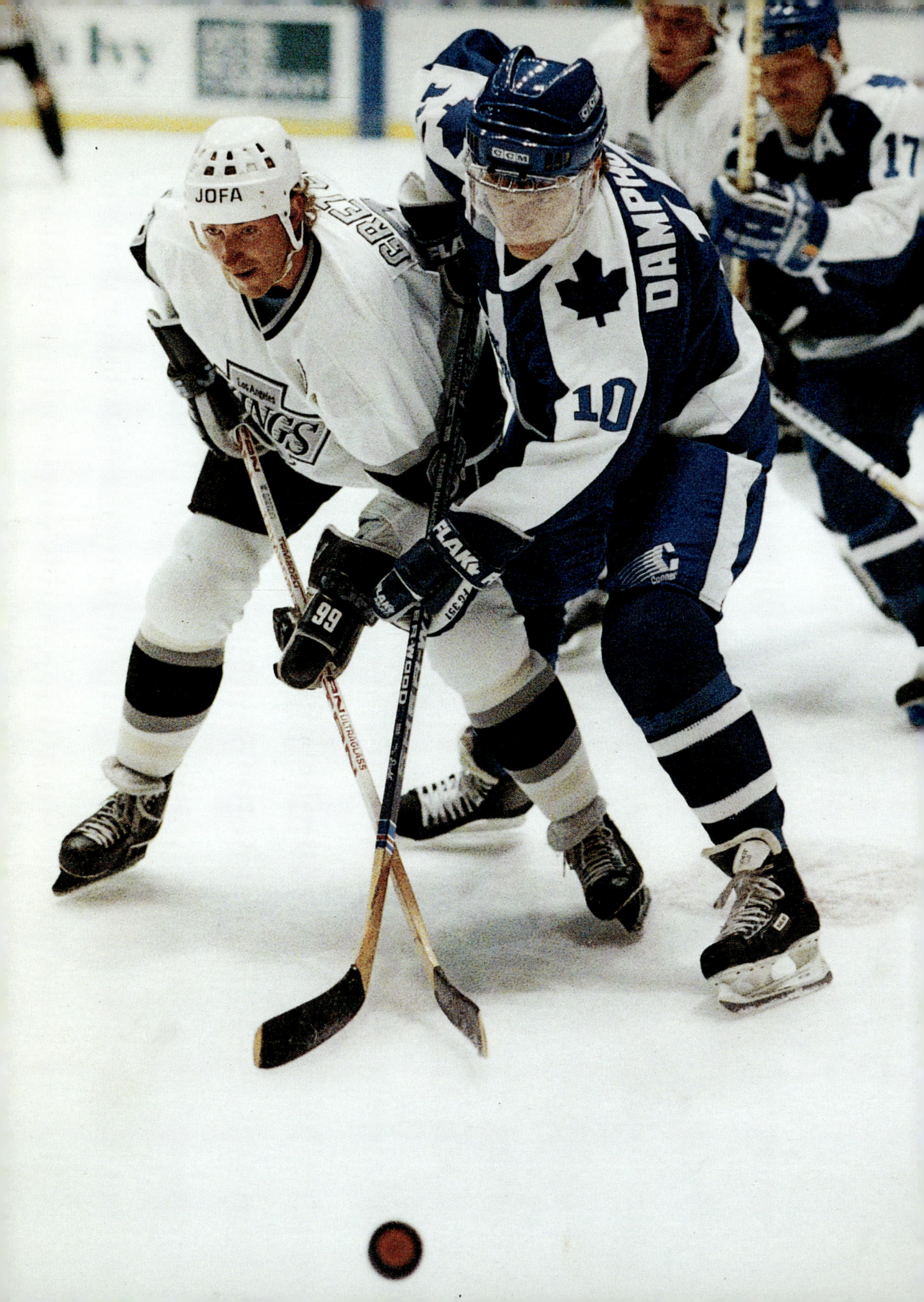
JOFA
CCM
10
17
99
Los Angeles
ULTRAGLASS

Gretzky, left, and the Toronto Maple Leafs' Vincent Damphousse fight for a loose puck.

1992–93 playoffs began, however, Gretzky showed everyone he was still a superstar. He led the Kings into the finals, where they lost to Montreal.

Hockey has never had a player like Wayne Gretzky. He has scored more goals and made more assists than anyone who has ever played the game. He has led the league in scoring nine times. He was named the NHL's Most Valuable Player every year from 1980 to 1987. While playing for the Edmonton Oilers, Gretzky led the team to four Stanley Cup titles (the Stanley Cup goes to the league's champion).

Wayne Gretzky was special from the time he was born. At age two, he was already skating. By the time he was a teenager, he was already one of the top players in the NHL. In 1982, when he was only 21, *Sports Illustrated* magazine named Gretzky its Sportsman of the Year. During the 1981–82 season, he scored 92 goals, a record that still stands. Gretzky didn't care about records, though, he just wanted to win a championship.

In 1983, Gretzky led the Oilers to the Stanley Cup finals against the New York Islanders, but they were no match for the powerful New York team. The

Gretzky practices at full speed during a team workout.

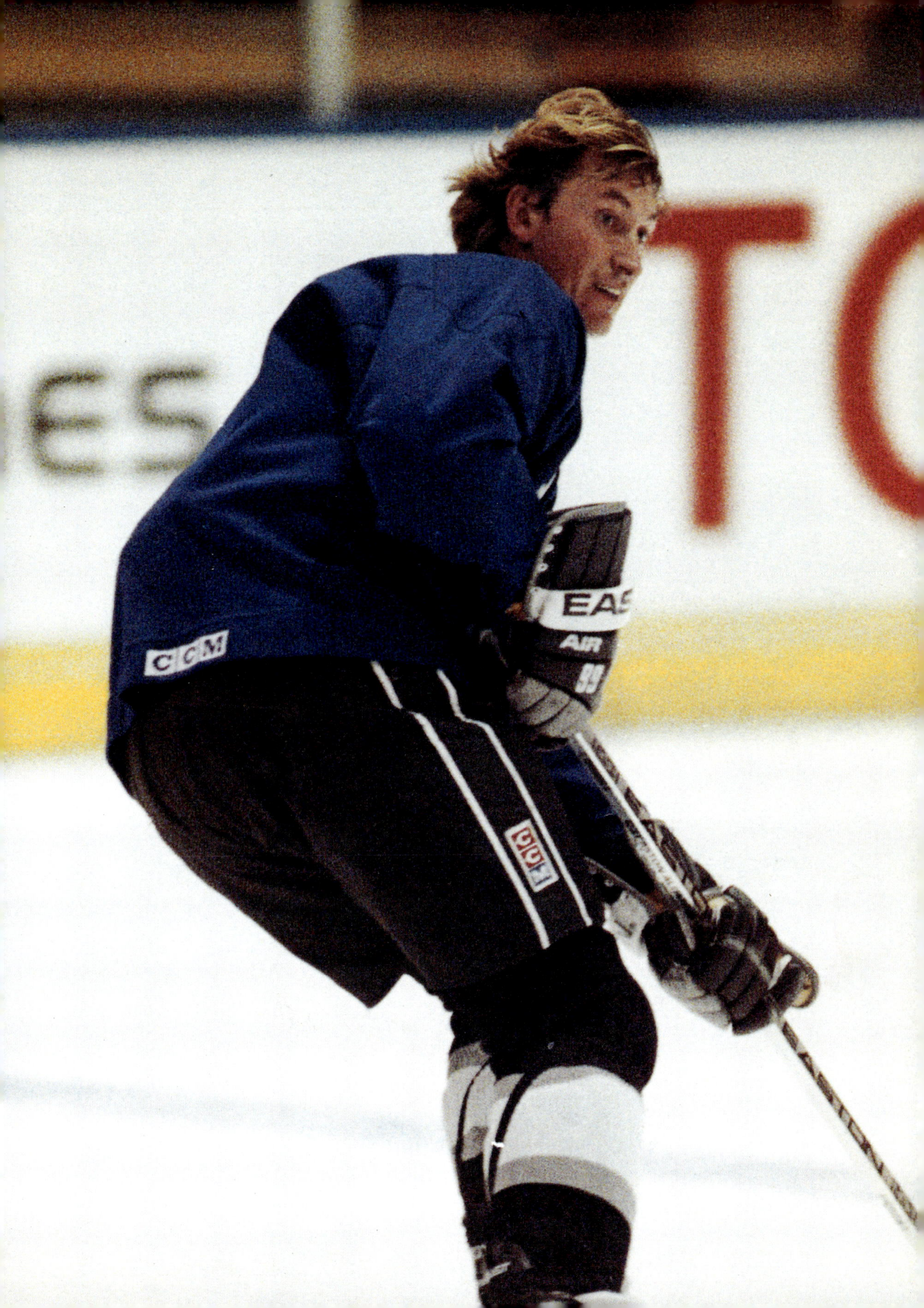
CCM

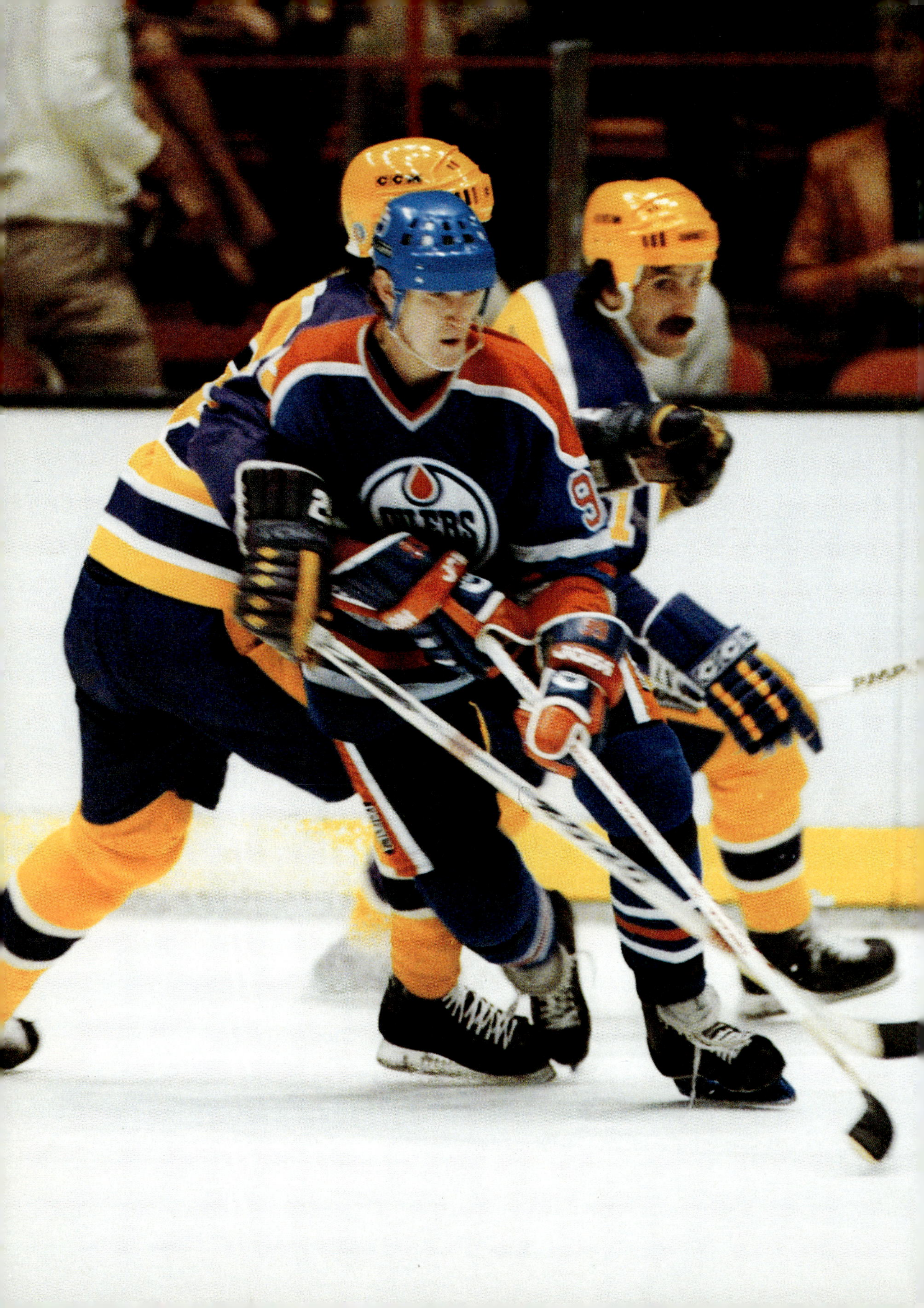
CCM

Wayne Gretzky skates for the Edmonton Oilers.

Islanders kept Gretzky from scoring even one goal in the series, and the Oilers went home without the Stanley Cup. The following year, Edmonton and New York met in the finals again. The Islanders had won four Stanley Cups in a row, but this time, it would be a different story.

Edmonton won two of the first three games of the series, but New York had kept Gretzky from scoring a goal. In fact, he hadn't scored against the Islanders for ten games. Gretzky was wondering if he would ever be able to put the puck in New York's net. He wouldn't have long to wait. In game four, Gretzky scored to give Edmonton a 1–0 lead. "That felt like the biggest goal of my career," he said after the game.

Gretzky got another goal as Edmonton won 3–1. The Oilers needed to take one more game to win the series. In game five, Gretzky led Edmonton to victory by scoring two goals. The greatest player in hockey history finally had his first Stanley Cup! After the game, each Edmonton player got to skate around the ice holding the cup. The first player to hold the Stanley Cup was Edmonton's captain, Wayne Gretzky.

The quest is over: Gretzky finally holds the Stanley Cup.

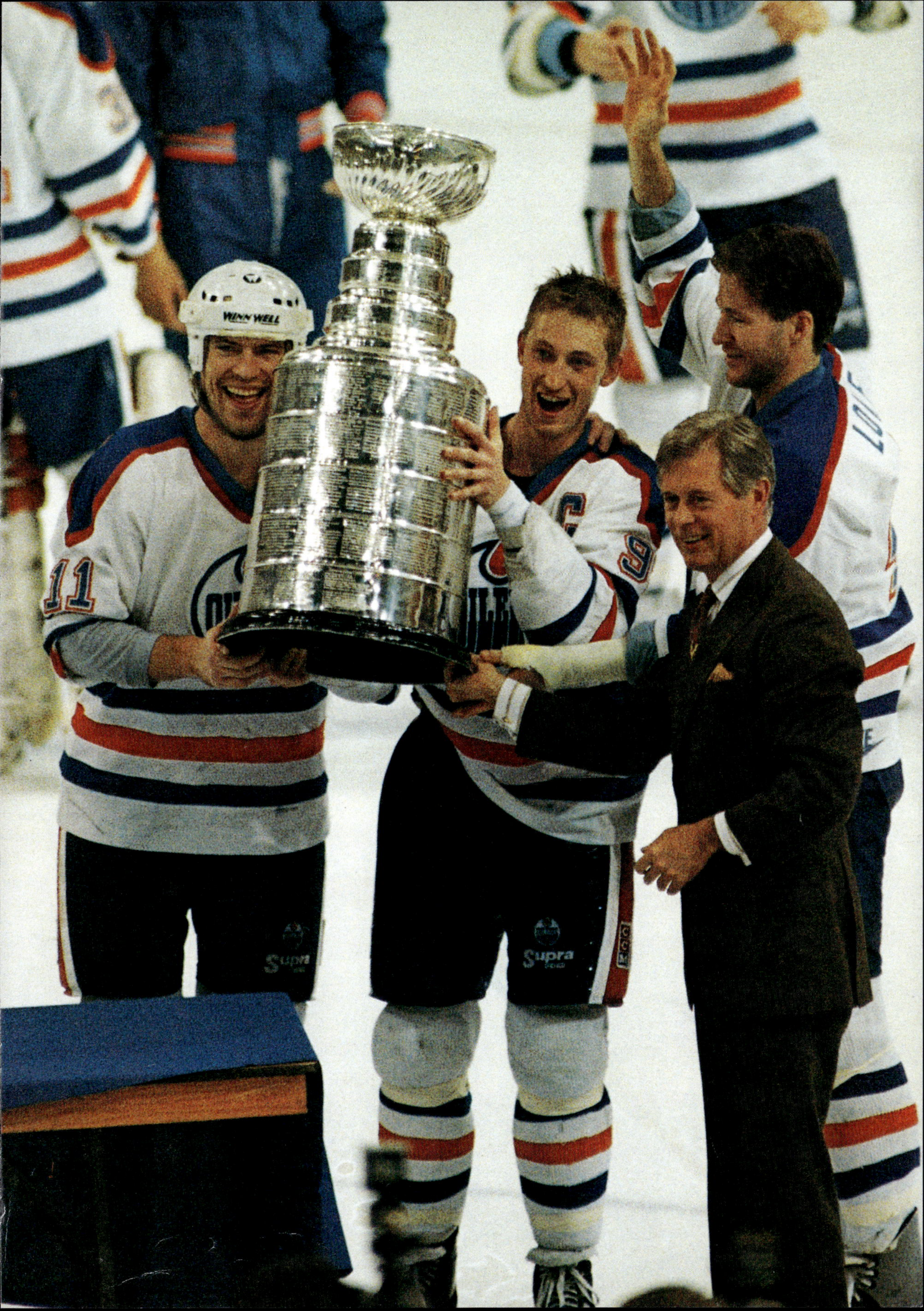
WINNWELL
Supra
Supra

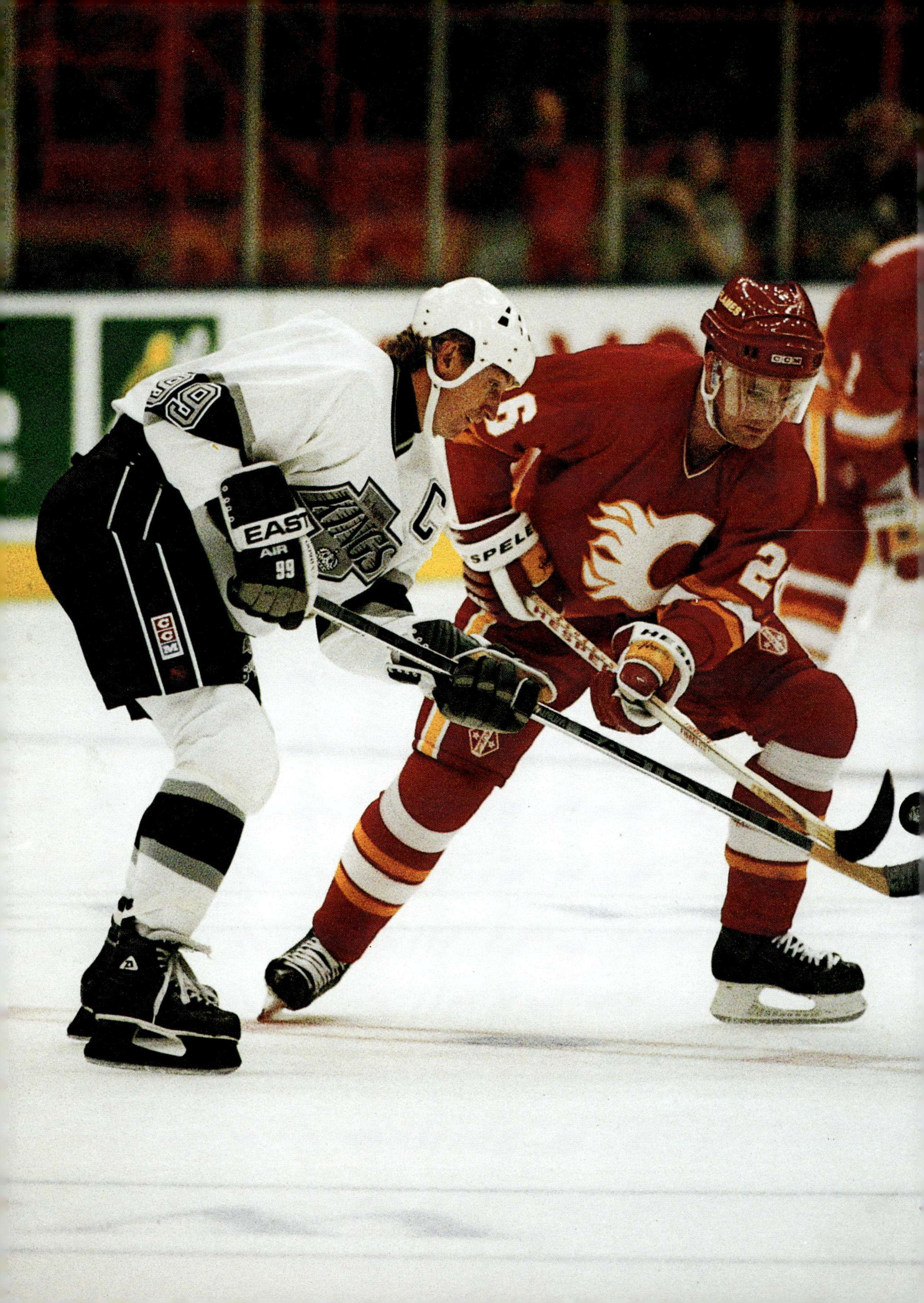
AIR
99
CCM

Gretzky (99) of the Los Angeles Kings battles Robert Reichel (26) of the Calgary Flames for the puck.

"You know," Gretzky said, "I've held women and babies. I've held jewels and money. But nothing will ever feel as good as holding that cup." Gretzky and the Oilers would get to hold the Stanley Cup again at the end of the 1984–85 season. Edmonton defeated the Philadelphia Flyers four games to one in the finals. Two years later, the Oilers and Flyers faced off again for the Stanley Cup, and Edmonton won three of the first four games.

Needing to take only one more game to win their third Stanley Cup in four years, the Oilers nearly blew it, losing games five and six. The winner of the seventh game would take the series and the cup. Despite losing two games in a row, the Oilers were confident. "By game time, we knew we were going to win," Gretzky said. "We could have played that game 20 times, and we would have won it 20 times."

Gretzky celebrates after scoring his 800th career goal.

L ed by Gretzky, the Oilers won game seven. The cup was theirs again! The next year, the Oilers got to hold the Stanley Cup for the fourth time in five years, when they beat the Boston Bruins in the 1987–88 finals, four games to none. Gretzky, however, had played his last game for Edmonton. He was traded to the

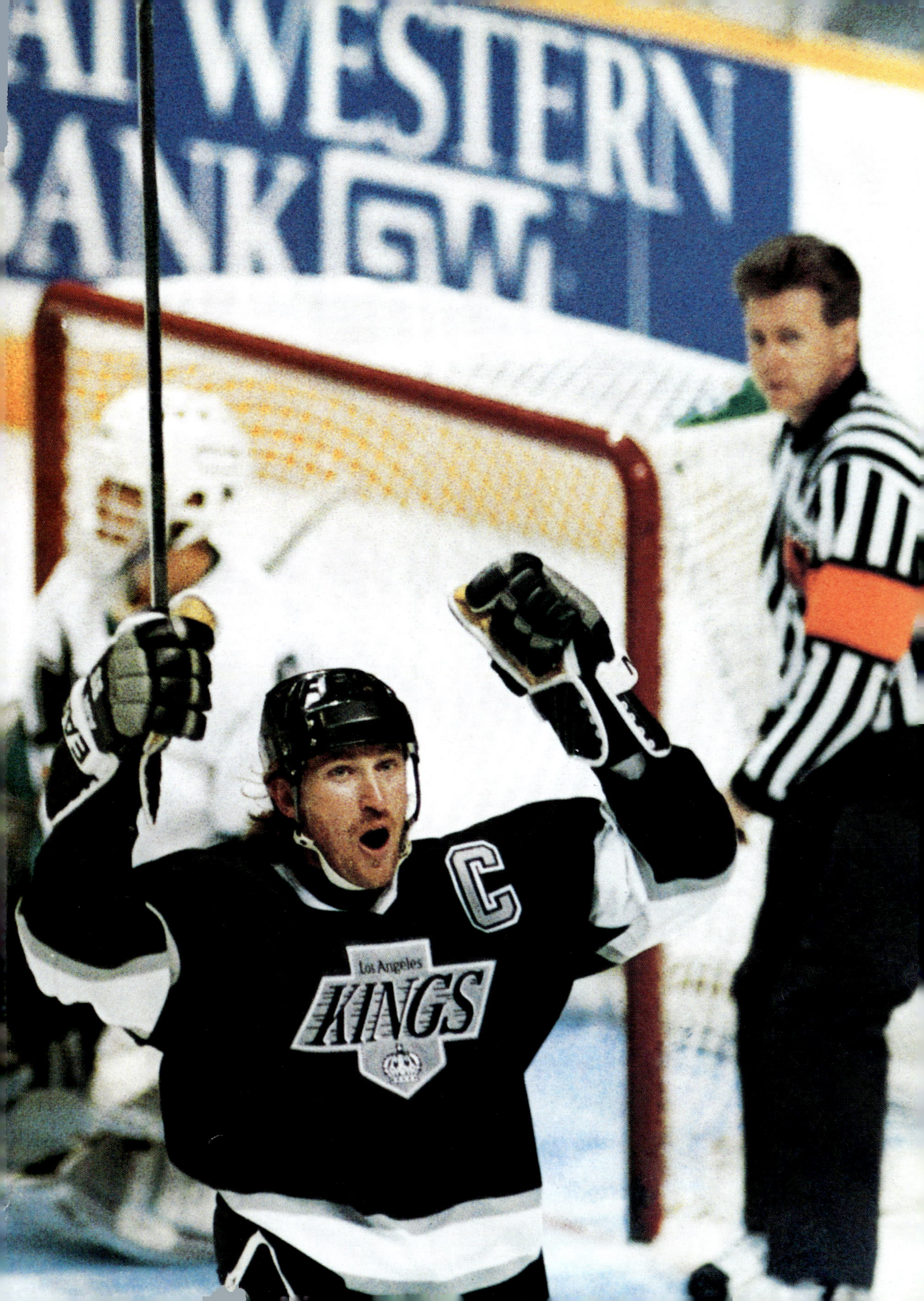
WESTERN
Los Angeles
KINGS

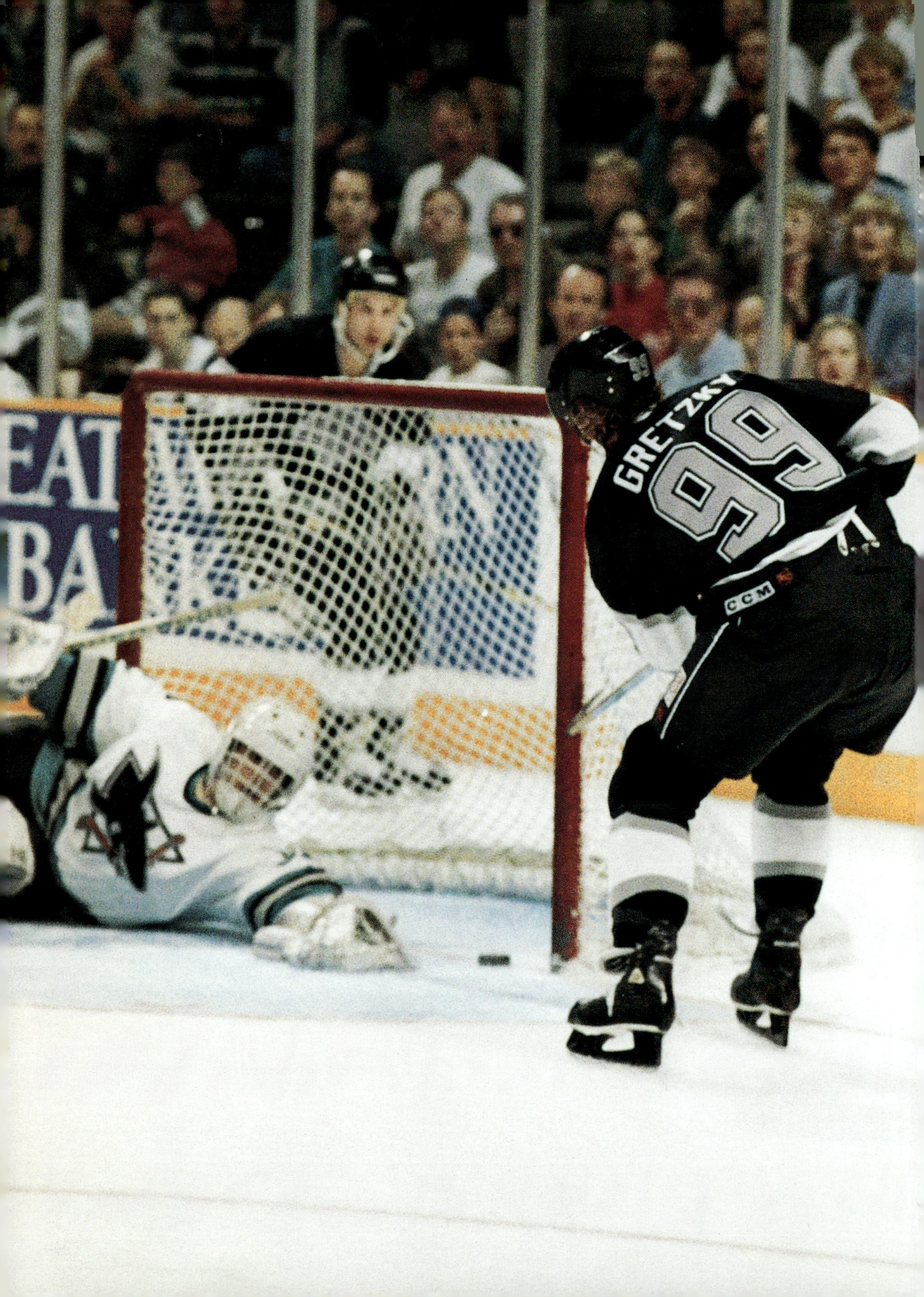
GRETZKY
99
CCM

Gretzky scores his 801st goal, tying Gordie Howe's record.

Los Angeles Kings before the 1988–89 season. In the playoffs that season, Gretzky and the Kings beat Edmonton.

During the 1989–90 season, Gretzky had a chance to break the scoring record of his idol, Gordie Howe. "When I was a kid," Gretzky said, "I wanted to play, talk, shoot, eat, laugh, look, and be like Gordie Howe." Gretzky did break Howe's record—and he did it in Edmonton. The Oiler fans gave their former star a long, long standing ovation. They stood and cheered for the best player ever. Wayne Gretzky truly was "The Great One."